live

laugh

love

play

this journal belong to:

_____

wake up!

begin each day as if it were on purpose.

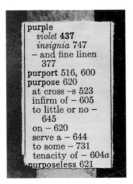

purple
violet **437**
insignia 747
– and fine linen
377
purport 516, 600
purpose 620
at cross –s 523
infirm of – 605
to little or no –
645
on – 620
serve a – 644
to some – 731
tenacity of – 604a
purposeless 621

an illustrated journal
art and words • mary anne radmacher

discover the
possibilities
which lie
within you in
order to live a
purposeful
life.

live with intention.
walk to the edge.
listen hard. play
with abandon.
practice wellness

risk love. continue to learn.

appreciate your friends

choose with no regret.

do what
you love.
Live as if this
is all there is.
mary anne radmacher

Intention.—N. intent, -ion
-ionality; purpose; *quo animo*; projec[t]
&c. 626; undertaking &c. 676; prede
termination &c. 611; design, ambition

contemplation, mind, *animus*, view
purview, proposal; study; look out.

final cause; *raison d'être*; *cui bon*[o]
object, aim, end; 'the be all and th[e]
end all'; drift &c. (*meaning*) 516
tendency &c. 176; destination, mark,
point, butt, goal, target, bull's-eye,
quintain; prey, quarry, game.

decision, determination, resolve; set
–, settled- purpose; *ultimatum*; resolu
tion &c. 604; wish &c. 865; *arrière
pensée*; motive &c. 615.

some
days
are
simply
meant
for
playing.

calculated
mischief
is
invigorating.

plays

mary anne radmacher

He had told them all not to speak to me under pain of disinheritance. I couldn't stop thinking about Meghan. I have learned to follow my instincts so I dialed Amsterdam. She was just about to kill herself — so depressed and jump five floors into the canal. Stop — hold on, I said — please don't do anything. I'm going to get you some help. I'll call you with tomorrow about this time. Promise me you won't do anything. I hung up the phone and called my shrink, explained the situation and the issues. The best place in the United States for her to go, given her issues, is the Meadows in Wickenburg, Arizona. I called Meghan back immediately and gave her the phone number. She was so desparate and lonely. She called right away and made a reservation at the first opening. My therapist said she belonged in treatment in this country — its her country and her primary language. Her mother and uncle had seen to it that she be removed from two art foundation boards; now her income was cut in half. I, in spite of the reality of $300,000 in legal bills standing up to her father in an attempt to divorce him, sent her a check for the first week in rehab. We thought a week would solve things. The Meadows said they needed her for at least a month as she was too close to killing herself. The cost was $30,000. I said somehow I would get the money for her. She said, it was her family issues that brought her there and that she would ask her parents for the money. We (I) decided that to protect her there was no reason for them to know of my involvement.

Plans

V. be -frier lly &c. *adj.*, − friends &
890, − acquainted with &c. *adj.*; kno
have the ear of; keep company w
munication −, have dealings −,
to; bear good will &c. (*benevolen*
of; befriend &c. (*aid*) 707; intr
set one's horses together hol
-friendship, − fellowship; come
&c. 892 with; break the ice, be
scrape- acquaintance with; get in
shake hands with, fraternize, en
throw oneself into the arms of; me

Adj. friendly; amic-able, -al; well
brotherly, fraternal, sisterly, syn
cordial, warm-hearted, devoted.

mary anne radmacher

home *focus* 74
   habitation 1?
   near 197
   interior 221
   arrival 292
   refuge 666
at – *party* 7?
   present 186
   within 221
   at ease 705
   social gather
    892
be at –
– *to visitors* 8?
feel at –
   freedom 748
   pleasure 82
   content 831
look at – .
   accusation 9.
make oneself
   free 748
   sociable 892
not be at – 7?
stay at – 265
at – in
   knowledge 49?
   skill 698
at – with

share ——— your heart

as deeply as you can reach.

worship 990
home *focus* 74
  habitation 1
  near 197
  interior 221
  arrival 292
  refuge 666
at – *party* 72
  present 186
  within 221
  at ease 705
  social gather
  892
be at –
  – *to visitors* 89
feel at –
  freedom 748
  pleasure 82
  content 831
look at –
  accusation 9
make oneself
  free 748
  sociable 892
not be at – 76
stay at – 265
at – in
  knowledge 490
  skill 698
at – with
  friendship

to favour, gain the friendship of.
   brace; receive with open arms,
   et half way, take in good part.
   affected, unhostile, neighbourly,
   pathetic, harmonious, hearty,

may every
room
hold laughter
and
every window
open to
great
possibility.

mary anne radmacher

some days there
aren't any
   trumpets ...
just lots of
dragons.

courage
doesn't always
roar.
   sometimes
courage is the
      quiet
       voice
at the end of
   the day saying,
"I will try
again
  tomorrow. "

mary anne radmacher

may all your
endeavors be rooted in
contentment and peace.

it is not the words
themselves but the
thought you take of
    the words
which creates

the
grand
adventure_____.
don't be a tourist be an
adventurer_____.
mary anne radmacher

boodle 793
book *register* 86
publication 531
   record 551
   volume **593**
   script 599
   enter accounts 811
at one's –s 539
bring to –
   evidence 467
   account 811
   reprove 932
mind one's – 539
school – 542
without –
   by heart 505
   – of Books 985
   – club 593
   – of fate 601
   – learning 490
   – shop 593
book-case 191
booked *dying* 360
bookish 490
bookkeeper 553
bookkeeping 811
bookless
   unlearned 493
bookmaking 156
bookselle
bo

mary anne radmacher

world

i am not the same
having seen the
moon shine on the
other side of the world.

may you be blessed

in knowing the love which surrounds you.

may you be safe in the sense of

place you have in your home.

may you be well in your body

and fortified in

the growing of
your spirit.

may your many
strengths and
the ⬭ wishes of
your loved ones
guide you in
⬭ all your days.

may your sleep be protected and sweet

mary anne radmacher

May your every day dawn with purpose and promise.

966. [Means of safety.] **Refuge.**—N.
refuge, sanctuary, retreat, fastness;
stronghold, keep, last resort; ward;
prison &c. 752; asylum, ark, home,
almshouse, refuge for the destitute;
hiding-place &c. (ambush) 530; sanctum
sanctorum &c. (privacy) 893; cache.

roadstead, anchorage; breakwater,
mole, port, haven; harbour, – of refuge;
sea-port; pier, jetty, embankment,
quay.

Content.—N. content,
-edness; complacency, satisfac-
tire satisfaction, ease, hea
peace of mind; serenity &

mary anne radmacher

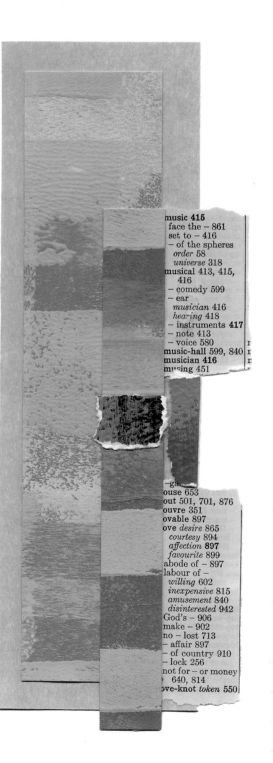

there are many ways

to listen to the music of love

wonder

love truly

love knows

so many roads . . . .

what joy there is
when one gets to
take part in the
song of love
itself :

as you walk may
angels gather at your
shoulder

play as often as you can.

V. be -courageous &c. *adj.*; dare, venture, make bold; face –, front –, affront –, confront –, brave –, defy –, despise –, mock- danger; look in the face; look -full, – boldly, – danger- in the face; face; meet, – in front; brave, beard; defy &c. 715.

take –, muster –, summon up –, pluck up- courage; nerve oneself, take heart; take –, pluck up- heart of grace; hold up one's head, screw one's courage to the sticking place; come -to, – up to- the scratch; stand, – to one's guns, – fire, – against; bear up, – against; hold out &c. (*persevere*) 604a.

put a bold face upon; show –,

V. be -courageous &c. *adj.*; dare, venture, make bold; face -, front -, affront -, confront -, brave -, defy -, despise -, mock- danger; look in the face; look -full, - boldly, - danger- in the face; face; meet, - in front; brave, beard; defy &c. 715.

take -, muster -, summon up -, pluck up- courage; nerve oneself, take heart; take -, pluck up- heart of grace; hold up one's head, screw one's courage to the sticking place; come -to, - up to- the scratch; stand, - to one's guns, - fire, - against; bear up, - against; hold out &c. (*persevere*) 604a.

put a bold face upon; show -,

mary anne radmacher

live

laugh

love ____

play

live boldly.
banish
loudly.
love truly.
play as often as you can.
work smart as
you are able.
share your heart
as deeply as you can reach.

as you awaken may
your dreams greet you
by name & may you
answer, "yes!"

as you walk may
angels gather at your
shoulder and may
you know they stand
with you.

as you rest
may all your
endeavors be rooted in
contentment and peace.

if you wonder
   look
   in their eyes;
if you are uncertain
   listen
   to their laughter.
if you feel inadequate
   feel
   their arms around
   you.
mother and father,
   both,
you are the
   stars
in their night sky.
as they
   grow you
   will become
the wind in
their sails

V. be -friendly &c. *adj.*, – friends &
890, – acquainted with &c. *adj.*; kno
have the ear of; keep company w
munication –, have dealings –,
to; bear good will &c. (*benevolen*
of; befriend &c. (*aid*) 707; intr
set one's horses together hold
-friendship, – fellowship; become
&c. 892 with; break the ice, be
scrape- acquaintance with; get int
shake hands with, fraternize, en
throw oneself into the arms of; me
Adj. friendly; amic-able, -al; well
brotherly, fraternal, sisterly, syn
cordial, warm-hearted, devoted.

mary anne radmacher

as you write

write to make sense of life experiences.
write to learn as much as you can from all the challenges and the joys.
write because words and ideas are fascinating.
write because exploring concept is play.
write to synthesize these explorations and make them practical.
write to become the best version of yourself.
write to empower others...and in the process empower yourself.
write to inspire, motivate, comfort, facilitate, discover, communicate.

in this scratching, this making marks...
encourage others to make their own mark.
(writing is therefore not simply an internal exercise but a way to
make a difference in the world)

write to define the truth ofyour life.
write to come clear on the intent of your heart.
write to wake up and sleep well.

write to wake up

as you write...
speak as truly and directly as your heart will allow.

as you write...
dream as largely and widely as your spirit can imagine.

as you write...

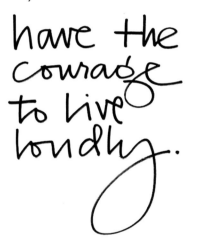
have the
courage
to live
loudly.

mary anne radmacher

About maryanne radmacher...

Primarily a writer - with a passion for color, design and form.
Her original writings partner with her artwork,
which visually represents and accents her words.

She's created her own lettering style, now associated with her compositions.

Based in Salem, Oregon, Mary Anne is committed to positive change in the world
and environmental responsibility.

www.maryanneradmacher.com

i am not the same
having seen the
moon shine on the
other side of the world.

All artwork and words by maryanne radmacher.
Book design by Liz Kalloch.